The Process

NAVIGATING THE CRIMINAL JUSTICE SYSTEM

Wendy B. Sellars

Publishing Advantage Group
www.PublishingAdvantageGroup.com

First Printing, 2017

ISBN: 154405369X
ISBN-13: 978-1544053691

DEDICATION

This book is dedicated to my awesome family and friends. For always supporting me and helping me to become the person I am today. To my husband, who I love with everything I am, thank you for allowing me to do what God has called me to do which is to work with people. Thank you to my children Khianna, Jocelin, Travis and Trinity for being my biggest supporters. Thank you for always understanding my vision and my dedication to work within my community. To the community of Thomasville NC thank you for your support and encouragement during this process of writing this book.

"Where justice is denied, where poverty is enforced, where ignorance prevails, and where any one class is made to feel that society is an organized conspiracy to oppress, rob and degrade them, neither persons nor property will be safe"

Frederick Douglas

CONTENTS

ACKNOWLEDGMENTS

I would like to express my gratitude to the many people who helped me while writing this book; to all those who provided support, talked with me about my ideas, and supported my passion for this topic.

I would like to thank my Lord and Savior Jesus Christ for giving me the wisdom, vision, desire and dedication to want to help others.

I would like the North Carolina Department of Public Safety, The Division of Adult Probation and Parole and my co-workers for all the training, knowledge and support which I have been afforded over the past 20 years. I would like to thank my mother Laura Bryant for encouraging me to publish this book. Above all, I want to thank my family who supported and encouraged me every step of the way.

"Every social justice movement that I know of has come out of people sitting in small groups, telling their life stories, and discovering that other people have shared similar experiences".

Gloria Steinem

The Process

NAVIGATING THE CRIMINAL JUSTICE SYSTEM

I have had the opportunity to work for the Department of Public safety for over 20 years. I started my career in 1995 working as a Corrections officer and moved to Probation and Parole in 2004. I have learned and encountered many different situations during my career and have come in contact with many different people since my start in 1995. What I have learned and experienced I have always tried to share with individuals who are not as informed. The system has several aspects to it and it takes an informed individual to navigate the process. This book was written to give the reader basic information from the initial law enforcement stops to an individual being sentenced to prison or probation. I hope it gives you the reader some insight on what to do when you find yourself or a loved one in the system.

Notes

_____

_____

_____

_____

_____

_____

_____

_____

_____

_____

_____

_____

_____

NOTES

_____

_____

_____

_____

_____

_____

_____

_____

_____

_____

_____

_____

_____

_____

_____

_____

_____

_____

_____

_____

_____

_____

_____

_____

_____

_____

_____

_____

_____

_____

The Stop

All law enforcement officers must have probable cause to stop you. Whether it is a broken tail light or you crossing the yellow line in your car, there must be a reason to stop you or your vehicle. Once the stop has been made it is wise to listen and adhere to the officer's instructions. Although you may feel the stop is unjustified it is best to stay calm, listen to the officer's reasoning and then calmly ask your questions. I suggest you get the officer's name and badge number in case you feel like further investigation is needed. If you are in a car always place your hands on the steering wheel until approached by the LEO. When you first see the blue lights and hear the sirens and you know that you will be stopped, this is the time to start gathering your information. The LEO will always ask for your license and registration.

I suggest when in your vehicle to always have your registration and your driver's license placed somewhere close to you for easy access. While driving always place your information in your middle console, glove box or "my favorite" over your driver side visor. This will ensure that you do not have to dig into your pocketbook or your back pocket in order to locate this information. Remember that the LEO will always need to see your hands in order for him or her to feel safe. They have initiated this encounter, but at this point, they don't know what your intentions are and they want to ensure their and your safety at all times.

Next, find a safe, well-lit and populated place to stop your vehicle. This ensures your safety and will encourage the individual that has stopped you to be more conscious of their actions and it should also help them feel safe. Again, if this location is not visible please slow your car down to between 20-25 mph and turn on your flashers. This should alert the officer that you acknowledge his presence behind you and that you are not trying to flee. Your speed and flashers are extremely important. If you want more protection call 911 and advise them of your situation.

Give them your name, description of the vehicle and your location, if known. Let the operator or dispatcher on the line know that you are being pulled over, but you are looking for a safe place to do so. The 911 operator should, in turn, alert the office or State Trooper of your intentions.

NOTES

_____
_____
_____
_____
_____
_____
_____
_____
_____
_____
_____
_____
_____
_____
_____
_____
_____
_____
_____
_____
_____
_____
_____
_____

"Justice has nothing to do with what goes on in a courtroom; Justice is what comes out of a courtroom".

Clarence Darrow

Probable Cause

"Probable cause" generally refers to the requirement in criminal law that police have adequate reason to stop, arrest, conduct a search, or seize property relating to an alleged crime.

The probable cause requirement comes from the Fourth Amendment to the U.S. Constitution, which states that:

"The right of the people to be secure in their persons, houses, papers, and effects, against unreasonable searches and seizures, shall not be violated, and no Warrants shall be issued, but upon probable cause, supported by Oath or affirmation, and particularly describing the place to be searched, and the persons or things to be searched."

As seen in those words, in order for a court to issue a warrant -- for someone's arrest, or to search or seize property -- there must be "probable cause."

The police must also have probable cause to arrest without a warrant, and in many cases to search or seize property without a warrant.

Prosecutors must also have probable cause to charge a defendant with a crime.

Warrants and Probable Cause:

Typically, to obtain a warrant, an officer will sign an affidavit stating the facts as to why probable cause exists to arrest someone, conduct a search or seize property. Judges issue warrants if they agree that probable cause exists.

There are many instances where warrants are not required to arrest or search; such as arrests for felonies witnessed in public by an officer. Here is more information on when warrants are not required.

If a warrantless arrest occurs, probable cause must still be shown after the fact and will be required in order to prosecute a defendant.

Probable Cause for Arrest:

Probable cause for arrest exists when facts and circumstances within the police officer's knowledge would lead a reasonable person to believe that the suspect has committed, is committing, or is about to commit a crime.

Probable cause must come from specific facts and circumstances, rather than simply from the officer's hunch or suspicion.

"Detentions" short of arrest do not require probable cause. Such temporary detentions require only "reasonable suspicion." This includes car stops, pedestrian stops and detention of occupants while officers execute a search warrant. "Reasonable suspicion" means specific facts which would lead a reasonable person to believe criminal activity was at hand and further investigation was required.

Detentions can turn into arrests, and the point where that happens is not always clear. Sometimes an officer will state that they are arresting a person, placing him/her in physical restraints, or might take other action crossing the line into arrest. These police actions may trigger the constitutional requirement of probable cause.

Someone arrested or charged without probable cause may file a civil lawsuit for false arrest or malicious prosecution.

Probable Cause to Search:

Probable cause to search exists when facts and circumstances known to the officer provide the basis for a reasonable person to believe that a crime was committed at the place to be searched, or that evidence of a crime exists at the location.

Search warrants must specify the place to be searched, as well as items to be seized.

There are many instances where a search warrant is not required. Common situations in which police are allowed to search without a warrant include the following:

1. When they have consent from the person in charge of the premises (although who that person is can be a tricky legal question);
2. When conducting certain searches connected to a lawful arrest; and
3. In emergency situations which threaten public safety or the loss of evidence.
4. Police also do not need a warrant to search or seize contraband which is "in plain sight" when the officer has a right to be present.

Probable Cause to Seize Property:

Probable cause to seize property exists when facts and circumstances known to the officer would lead a reasonable person to believe that the item is contraband, is stolen, or constitutes evidence of a crime.

When a search warrant is at play, police generally must search only for the items described in the warrant. However, any contraband or evidence of other crimes they come across may, for the most part, be seized as well.

Should evidence prove to have resulted from an illegal search, it becomes subject to the "exclusionary rule" and cannot be used against the defendant in court. After hearing arguments from the prosecuting and defense attorneys, the judge decides whether evidence should be excluded.

Probable cause refers to the amount and quality of information required to arrest someone, to search or seize private property in many cases, or to charge someone with a crime. Probable cause to arrest, searches, or seize property exists when facts and circumstances known to the police officer would lead a reasonable person to believe the following:

1. That the person to be arrested has committed a crime;
2. That the place to be searched was the scene of a crime;
3. That the place to be searched contains evidence of a crime; and/or
4. That property to be seized is contraband, stolen, or constitutes evidence of a crime.

The 4th Amendment

The right of the people to be secure in their persons, houses, papers, and effects, against unreasonable searches and seizures, shall not be violated, and no Warrants shall issue, but upon probable cause, supported by Oath or affirmation, and particularly describing the place to be searched, and the persons or things to be seized.

Plain View Search

A police officer may seize an object which he believes to be the instrumentality of a crime if the object is in plain view and these three conditions are met:

the officer was lawfully in the location where he viewed the object;

the officer had lawful access to the object; and

the object's incriminating nature was immediately apparent – that is, simply by viewing the object, the officer had probable cause to believe it was contraband, without the need for any further search of the object.

NOTES

The Search

You are now pulled over by LEO and you have provided your requested information. Again, you should always keep your hands on the steering wheel. Always remain calm although I know it is hard to even when you have done nothing wrong. Understand that if you are like most this is not an everyday occurrence for you. With all the stories in the media today this situation can be gut wrenching, but try your best to breathe and do not make any sudden moves. Always stay calm, breath and ask permission to do anything. At this point, the officer will begin on his or her investigation. You will be asked several questions; such as your whereabouts and where you might be headed. If the LEO feels like they have probable cause to stop you, they will possibly call for back up and ask to search your car or your person. At this point, you have two options (1) to allow the search (2) not to allow the search. This decision is totally up to you. Take into consideration that option two will take a lot longer because at this point the process of obtaining a search warrant will begin. The process of obtaining a warrant starts with the request, then approval by a supervisor and lastly approval by and signature of a district court judge. Once all required steps and signatures have been obtained it will go back to the officer who initiated the stop and the search will begin. Understand that you are allowed to be present during this entire search process. Normally if you are the driver of the car what is found in the car will be viewed as your possession. If you are a passenger in a car and contraband is found and it is in arm's reach of your seat you can be charged with it.

As for your person, an LEO can perform a frisk or a pat down but must have your permission unless you are temporarily detained or under arrest. Of course, anything on your person will be charged to you.

Your home is also a searchable entity, but like your car, the LEO must have your permission to search it. The two options you have are the same as with a vehicle stop and the process to obtain a warrant is also the same.

You are again allowed to be present during the search by LEO's.

The one side note to any search by a Law Enforcement Officer is that if an individual is on Active Probation or Post release a search can be conducted at any time without an individual's permission. The search must be conducted by the individual's Probation/Post-release Officer and no probable cause is needed. This type of search can be carried out because it is a condition of probation and post-release. The individual being supervised can and must submit to the warrant-less searches at any time by their supervision officer. Anyone placed on these two types of supervision sign documents giving permission to search.

NOTES

The Arrest

The stop has been made; the search has been conducted and now due to paraphernalia or evidence found the arrest is underway. Again I stress stay calm during this whole process. There is no argument, foul language or combative actions that will derail the process once it has started. Try your best to remember names of officers and what is said to you. Pay close attention to words like detained and arrested because there is a huge difference. And what is the difference you may ask?

When an LEO tells you that you are detained this mean that your freedom is not obstructed. This means that you can leave if you want and you have not been moved from one location to another. I don't suggest that you just walk away if you are being detained, but I would suggest in a calm manner asking why you are being detained.

When an LEO tells you that you are under arrest this starts a whole life changing set of events. The first step and most important step in this process are having the arresting officer read you your Miranda rights.

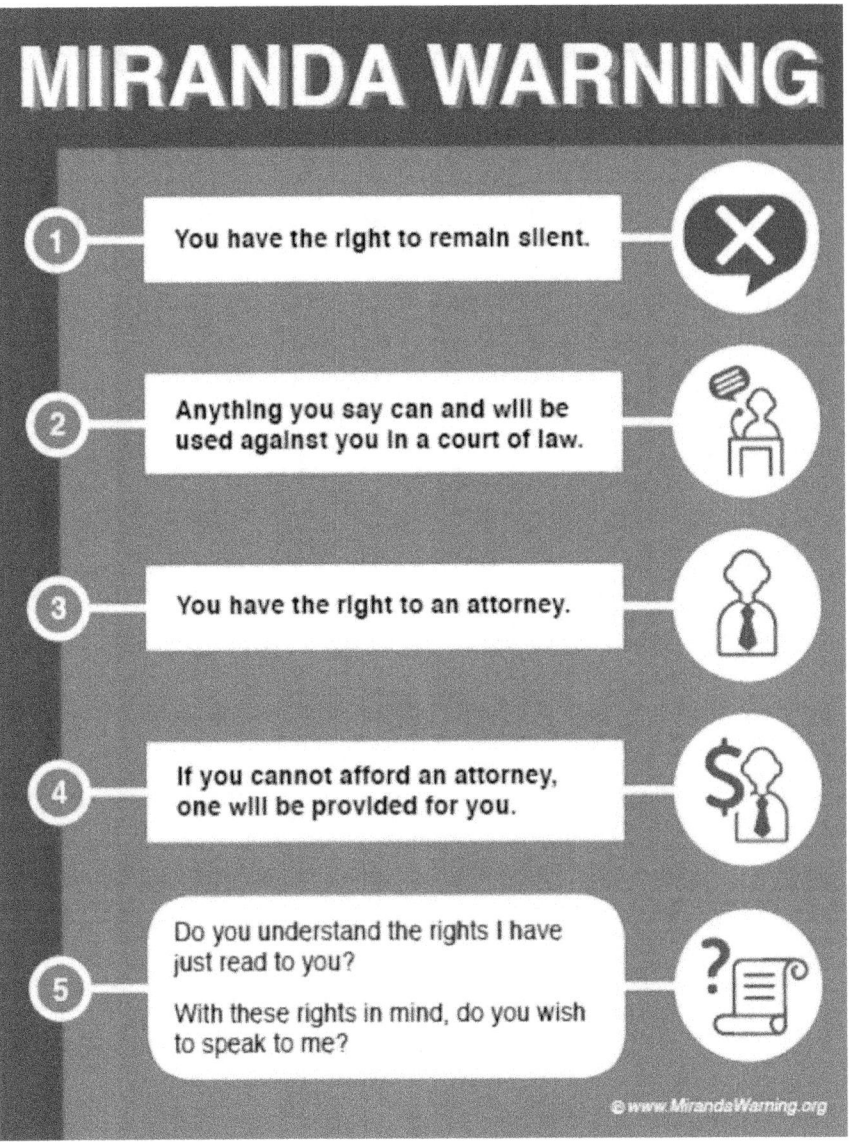

This is what must happen to start the process and the most important right of Miranda is "You have the right to remain silent and ANYTHING you say can and will be used against you in a court of law". And when they say anything they mean anything!

Now, the decision to make a statement is totally up to you, but you must remember that you are probably being videotaped and recorded. Once you make a statement there are is no recanting what you have said. So if you are unsure of the Process or what you can or cannot say I suggest you please ask for an attorney. As part of Miranda, the system will provide an attorney for you if you can't afford to provide one for yourself. So, with that being said, in the state of North Carolina, you are required to have a first appearance 24 hours after being arrested. So if you are arrested, questioned and you ask for an attorney the interview must stop at that point.

Once the interview stops you will be walked or transported to the magistrate's office. The magistrate's job is to advise you of what you are being charged with, give you a bond and give you your next court date. Your bond will be determined by the crime you are being accused of, prior criminal record and your demeanor during the arrest. This is another reason to be calm and as non-combative as possible. If the stop, search and interview result in an arrest the LEO has a lot of influence on your bond. Even though it is up to the magistrate to set your bond, don't take that interaction for granted.

Once your bond is set there are several ways that it can be posted Cash, bond or property. Bail bonds help to assure a person's appearance in court. A person who has been arrested for an offense and placed under a "secured bond" may be released from custody by putting up the full amount of the bond in cash, with the signature of a person who has enough property to cover the amount of the bond, or by a bail agent. Bail agents charge a non-refundable fee of up to 15 percent of the amount of the bond. Upon signing the bond, the bail agent becomes responsible for the defendant's appearance in court and liable for the full amount of the bond. If the defendant appears in court as required and the case is disposed of, the bond is void. If the defendant fails to appear in court, the bail agent must return the defendant to the court within 150 days or pay the full amount of the bond. This provides a strong financial incentive for the bail agent to do his or her job.

If a bail agent is forced to forfeit on a bond, the bond amount is paid directly to North Carolina's free public school system.

The setting of a bail bond is a way for the court to ensure that a person obligated to appear in court will do so. It also is supposed to protect the public from potentially dangerous defendants. The seriousness of the crime, prior criminal record, employment, family circumstances, and living situation can all play a role in making a bail bond decision.

When representing yourself, the way you explain your situation to the judge is very important in determining whether or not you await trial behind bars.

When facing a bond hearing, it is important to understand what exactly a bail bond is. A bail bond is essentially a legal contract that releases an individual from custody. Bail is the security that is given to the State in order for you to be released from jail. Bond is a legally binding obligation on the person posting bail to return for their scheduled court appearance. A secured bond requires that you or someone on your behalf puts up something of value to assure your appearance in court. Often, this amount is higher than the amount of money you have available to you. Ideally, you would like to receive an unsecured bond or written promise to appear, which does not require payment in order for you to be released from jail. The factors that help the court determine whether or not you are a danger or flight risk, along with your ability to explain the application of these factors to yourself, will decide whether or not you receive an unsecured or lower bond.

After a bond is set, you have the right to ask the court to lower your bail. This is done through a motion to modify bond. After filing, the motion a hearing can be granted in one or two ways: (1) by consent of the judge and the prosecutor, or (2) by a hearing in front of a judge, opposed by the prosecutor. You do not want to file a motion to modify in every situation. If a prosecutor feels that the bond is already set properly, having to argue against a motion could lead to the prosecutor asking for an increase in bail. For this reason, it is important to talk with someone if you think your bail is too high. A lawyer can inform you of the right circumstances to file a motion to modify.

At either the bail bond hearing or on a motion to modify bail, it can be important to have a lawyer who understands what needs to be said and who can aggressively fight to limit or reduce your bail bond. Understanding the bail process can be confusing at times, and reaching out to a lawyer can often help to increase your understanding and ease your concerns.

After your bond is set one of two things will occur, you will have the ability to post your bond or you will remain in custody. If you are not able to make bond right away hopefully you have opted to use your constitutional right to a court-appointed attorney. Court appointed attorneys sometimes have reputations for being ineffective. In many circumstances this is incorrect. In the very few instances where this might be true, you still need representation. If you are struggling to make bail I can promise you that you at this point can't afford to retain an attorney.

With an attorney and a court date in place now comes the next phase in your decision-making.

NOTES

_____

_____

_____

_____

_____

_____

_____

_____

_____

_____

_____

_____

_____

_____

_____

The Court Date

Your day in court is here and I am sure you are ready to get all this behind you, right? Well, let me be the bearer of bad news, our court system is not that swift. More than likely this is how your day in court will happen. First, you will appear in court and answer the docket.

Your Initial Appearance (Arraignment):

You should arrive 15 minutes before the time shown on your citation or summons.

The district attorney will advise you of what you have been charged with. He or she will also advise you of how much time you will face if found guilty. Don't panic when you hear this information. Usually, you will not receive the suggested amount of time because there are a lot of things that are taken into consideration by the judge before a sentence are given. It is the District Attorney's job to make sure they give you all the information pertaining to your case.

Charges and Possible Penalties:

The judge tells you the charge(s) and the possible penalties and asks if you understand them. The judge is asking only if you understand the charges; if you do not understand the charge or the possible penalties, tell the judge what you don't understand and the judge will explain.

If you have decided to hire or use a court appointed attorney they will explain all information about your case to you. Please make sure that you understand all information relayed to you by your attorney. If you do not understand any aspect of your case please ask questions. This information is very important and you need to make sure you understand what is going on. All attorneys do not have your best interest at heart. It is your responsibility to understand your case and take responsibility for the outcome of your case. More than likely your first court date will not be your last. After being arraigned you will be given another Court date.

This will give your attorney the opportunity to talk to the district attorney about your case.

Right to Counsel:

The judge asks if you want a lawyer. If you can't afford one, you can ask the judge for a court-appointed lawyer. If you ask for a court-appointed lawyer, you fill out a form or the judge asks questions about your finances to make sure you qualify. You may be required to reimburse the county for all or part of the costs of the court-appointed lawyer. A court-appointed lawyer is available only if jail time is possible.

Do You Need an Attorney?

You are not required to have an attorney. You may represent yourself if you wish.

If you would like to represent yourself or if you want a lawyer to represent you is a decision only you can make. North Carolina courts have tried to make it easier for people who want to represent themselves in court, particularly in misdemeanor cases.

Neither a judge, court clerk's or district attorney's office can give you legal advice.

If you have been charged with a felony, your court date will start out in district court. This is where all court cases start. Some felony case will then go to the grand jury. The grand jury plays an important role in the criminal process, but not one that involves a finding of guilt or punishment of a party. A prosecutor will work with a grand jury to decide whether to bring criminal charges or an indictment against a potential defendant. This is usually reserved for individuals with serious felonies. Grand jury proceedings are much more relaxed than normal courtroom proceedings. There is no judge present and frequently there are no lawyers except for the prosecutor. The prosecutor will explain the law to the jury and work with them to gather evidence and hear testimony. A grand jury has broad power to see and hear almost anything they would like.

All felony criminal cases, civil cases involving more than $25,000 and misdemeanor and infraction appeals from District Court are tried in Superior Court.

A jury of 12 will hear the criminal cases scheduled for trial. In the civil cases, juries are often waived.

So, just to be clear, District court is where misdemeanors are heard and Superior court is where felonies are heard.

Your case is now in the correct courtroom and is now ready to go before the judge.

The next decision you will have to make is whether or not you will plead guilty or innocent and whether or not you will take a plea bargain or go to trial.

The Plea - Guilty or Not Guilty?

The judge will ask if you would like to plead guilty or not guilty. If you are not sure whether you want to plead guilty or not guilty, you can ask the judge to reschedule your initial appearance so you can talk to an attorney first. You can also plead not guilty, and talk to an attorney before your next court date or simply leave it to the prosecution to try to prove its case.

Guilty Plea:

If you plead guilty, you are admitting you committed the offense charged. You are also giving up your right to a trial and your right to remain silent. If you plead guilty, the judge decides the sentence.

Not Guilty Plea - Court or Jury Trial?

If you plead not guilty, the judge will ask if you want a court trial or a jury trial. In a court trial, the judge hears the evidence and decides if you are guilty. In a jury trial, twelve members of the community serve as the jury, and they hear the evidence and decides if you are guilty. If you are found guilty after either a court trial or a jury trial, the judge decides the penalty (the sentence). A court trial usually takes less than an hour; a jury trial usually takes a full day or longer.

A plea bargain is an agreement between a defendant and a prosecutor, in which the defendant agrees to plead guilty or no contest (nolo contendere) in exchange for an agreement by the prosecutor to drop one or more charges, reduce a charge to a less serious offense, or recommend to the judge a specific sentence.

Plea bargains are used a lot by the district attorney's offices across the state. They are frequently used and the primary justifications for plea bargains are because the courts are overcrowded. If plea bargains were not utilized the court system would be overwhelmed and forced to shut down. Prosecutors' caseloads are also overloaded and plea bargains allow for fewer trials; which means that the prosecutor can more effectively prosecute the more serious cases. Please remember that just because a plea bargain is offered does not mean you have to take it. You have a constitutional right to take your case to trial. Sometimes District attorney's will use scare tactics to pressure a defendant into to taking these deals. I understand that when you are in jail with no signs of release these deals may seem like your only way out.

Please think long and hard about your decision because once it is signed and you enter into the agreement it is a done deal. Plea agreements usually come with its own set of requirements; which normally include fines, restitution, community service, treatment, probation or a combination. If you decide to take your case to trial, which should always be the case when you feel you are innocent, don't think that it will be a quick fix. Trial preparation can take months and sometimes years. Several hours will be invested in preparing for your trial, but if you are innocent it should be well worth the time. If you are still incarcerated during this process you are well within your rights to ask the court for a bond reduction and your attorney can assist you with this motion. If you are not in jail you should be actively helping your attorney prepare for your defense. Any information you can provide to your attorney will only help your defense.

You are now at the point in your journey where you will have to stand before the judge and possibly a jury to either hear the words case dismissed or you are guilty as charged.

Court Etiquette:

Appropriate dress is required in a courtroom. A great rule of thumb is to always dress like you are attending church or a job interview. It will make you look better in the eyes of a judge. If this type of attire is not available, make sure you wear clothing that looks presentable. No pajamas, short pants, low-cut blouses, pants with holes or rips in them or shirts with explicit language or references to anything illegal.

Food or drink is not allowed in any courtroom. Children should not be brought into a courtroom unless they are old enough to sit quietly and not disrupt the proceedings. Cell phones and all electronic devices should be turned off while you are in the courtroom. It is illegal to bring weapons of any kind into a courthouse.

If you are represented by a lawyer, listen

to his or her advice, and ask questions so that you understand what is happening and can make the best decisions for yourself. If you are not represented by a lawyer, make the effort to become familiar with the law and procedures involved in your case.

Please be patient. There may be a delay before your case is called, and there are a variety of reasons why delays happen. It is often necessary to schedule several hearings for the same time, to make the most efficient use of court time. Sometimes, a hearing scheduled earlier in the day takes longer than the court or the parties anticipated. Sometimes the court must deal with urgent matters (such as emergency child protection hearings or 50-B hearings) which take precedence over previously scheduled hearings.

Interpreters are available for participants who cannot speak, hear, or understand the English language. If an interpreter is needed in your case, contact the court clerk's office prior to your first appearance in court.

If you have been acquitted or found not guilty by the court congratulations, you are among an elite few. Hopefully, you will learn from this experience and try hard not to find yourself in this situation again. If you have been found guilty you will face two options, Incarceration or probation.

If you are sentenced to an active sentence it will be a life-changing experience.

Sentencing:

If you have pleaded guilty or are found guilty, the judge will decide your sentence. The judge will decide your sentence at the time you plead guilty or are found guilty. The judge will ask if there is anything you want to say before the judge decides your sentence. Your sentence is written in a judgment, and you are given a copy.

The sentence must be within the minimum and maximum limits set by statute. (The judge will have told you the potential penalties that apply in your case at your initial appearance.) Misdemeanor sentences can include jail, driver's license suspension, fines, court costs, community service, probation, and restitution (money paid to the victim to cover the costs for treatment of an injury or to repair or replace damaged or destroyed property - Restitution).

Payments are due, jail time starts, and driver's license suspensions start at the time of sentencing unless the judge allows otherwise.

If your judgment includes a deadline for future payments, it will also include a date and time for a review hearing. If you do not meet the deadlines, you must appear at the review hearing and show good cause why the court should not hold you in contempt. If the judge decides that you did not have good cause, the judge may require you to pay fines and/or serve jail time for contempt. The court is more likely to find good cause, and to allow an extension of the deadline if you have paid a significant portion of the amount due.

If your judgment includes a period of probation, and if you do not comply with the terms of probation, the prosecutor may file a motion asking the court to find that you have violated your probation. If the court finds you have violated probation, the court may order you to pay additional fines, serve additional jail time, or anything else the court have included at the original sentencing.

If your sentence includes a driver's license suspension, do not drive until you have a permit in your possession; once you have the permit, drive only during the times and for the purposes stated on the permit.

Appeal:

On appeal, the district court decides whether the magistrate judge in your case followed the proper procedures and properly applied all the applicable laws. Either you or the prosecutor may file an appeal within the court mandated days after the judgment is entered.

Failure to Appear:

If you do not appear for your initial appearance, you may be charged with an additional offense known as failure to appear (FTA). An FTA is a misdemeanor, punishable by up to six months in jail and/or a fine of up to $500, plus court costs. If you are charged with an FTA, the court is likely to issue a warrant for your arrest.

If you fail to appear for proceedings after your initial appearance, the court will likely issue a warrant for your arrest. You will be required to show good cause why the court should not hold you in contempt. If you are held in contempt, you may be required to pay fines and/or to serve time in jail.

If you can't appear at the scheduled time, contact your attorney or the court as soon as possible. If the court is contacted ahead of time and if you have a good reason, the court may reschedule your case. The court requires compelling reasons before it excuses a failure to appear.

What are you charged with?

There are three general types of offenses: *felonies* (which can be subject to term in a state prison), *misdemeanors* (which can be subject to up to one year in a county jail), and *infractions* (which can be subject to a fine up to $100.00, plus court costs). Procedures for the different categories are somewhat different.

Once you get to your assigned detention facility try your best to quickly get assigned to a work detail or an educational program. This will not only help you get through your sentence but it will keep you occupied mentally and physically. It will also allow you to possibly work days off of your sentence.

NOTES

Probation

The sentence of Probation can be a burden or it can be a blessing in your life. It really depends on where you are in the process. If you are bitter and not ready to take responsibility for your bad decisions, it will be your worst nightmare. On the other hand, if you are tired of being trapped in the system and finding yourself standing in a courtroom every other month, probation might be your way to a better life. It has always been said that your probation officer can be your best friend or your worst nightmare. So what can you expect if you are placed on probation? There are two kinds of probation, supervised and unsupervised. Supervised probation consists of you reporting to an officer as you are directed to do. Normally you will report once a month unless told otherwise. Unsupervised probation is when you have no officer to report to. You are given certain conditions to address like paying a fine, community service hours and staying out of trouble for the duration of your unsupervised term. Take for instance you are placed on unsupervised probation for 12 months. The court requires that you complete all conditions ordered and not receive any new charges for the duration of that unsupervised period (12 months). Supervised probation is a totally different animal. With supervised probation, you will be assigned a probation officer. This process will be started during intake; which happens before you leave court. Your officer will be assigned by county of residence, which means you must be supervised in the county you live in.

For example, if you live in Durham County and you receive a conviction in Wake County you will be supervised in Durham

County. Any and all conditions must be satisfied in the county of supervision except one. If you are ordered to pay any money like a fine, restitution, attorney's fee, supervision fee, etc. they must be paid in the county of conviction.

Conditions for Probation

- No new offenses (minor traffic violations excepted)
- No illicit drug use
- Restrictions on alcohol use/abuse
- Reporting to probation officer as required
- Paying required fees and fines
- Avoid contact with other offenders
- Follow all court orders

The state of North Carolina has implemented a system that allows you to pay these fees online.

Your probation officer can provide you with this information. Being placed on probation can be confusing and sometimes scary. It is a very intricate machine, but your officer is there to help you navigate through it. Probation officers are there to help and want you to successfully complete the process. The first 60 days of your probationary sentence is very important. This is the period where you and your officer will get to know each other. Your officer will have mandatory home visits and office visits that he or she has to conduct during the first sixty days. Along with theses contacts will come a risk needs assessment which will determine you criminogenic needs. This might sound bad, but it is actually a great tool that the department uses to help an officer know what areas you need the most help in. It's actually like being in school when you took certain assessments to determine what your strengths and weaknesses were in a particular subject. Your teacher gets the results of your test and it shows you are strong in division, but you are weak in fractions. There is no need in helping you with division because you already know that material. So the teacher will help you become stronger in fractions. It's the same concept with your RNA. If you are strong in mental health and weak in substance abuse guess what? Probation is going to focus on substance abuse because that is a weakness. This weakness can also be a life area that can cause you to commit a new offense. If you allow your officer to utilize the system in place and you work with the office you will be surprised the progress you can make. After the initial 60 days, your officer will determine what level you are. The leveling process is determined by your risk needs assessment. A person can level anywhere from a level 5 to a level 1. The numbers attached to these levels do not indicate bad or good. The levels are only used to determine how much or how little assistance you need from your officer. Level 5 is the lowest level of supervision you can have. Level 5 individuals are not required to report in to see an officer. They are however required to remote report; which is done electronically on a computer or smart phone. These individuals are still required to complete any conditions ordered by the court and must complete them by their supervision end date.

Individuals that are level 4 must report for a face-to-face contact with their officers every three months. These individuals are also required to complete any conditions ordered by the court and must have them completed by their supervision end date.

Level 3, 2 and 1 cases must report to their probation officer once every 30 days. Officers work very closely with this population to make sure that they are referred to and complete any conditions ordered by the court. Probation officers will take these individuals through the probation process step-by-step to answer any and all questions.

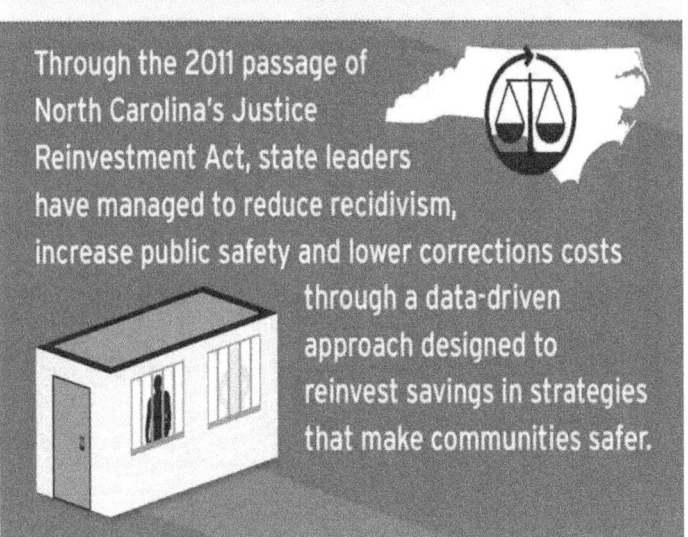

Probationary sentences can last anywhere from 6 months to 5 years and can be extended an additional 3 years for a total of 8 years. The length of the sentence is determined by and ordered only by the sentencing judge. Always remember when talking to your attorney or the assistant district attorney you want to ask if you qualify for a deferred prosecution or the 90-96 programs. Both of these programs are for first-time offenders and will allow you to keep your record free from convictions. What do I mean by that you might ask? To be labeled as a first-time offender means that you have not been convicted of any other criminal offense since the age of 16 years old. Please note that criminal offenses do not include traffic offenses you can be eligible for these programs.

So that is it the process, how to navigate the criminal justice system. I hope this information gives you the answers to some of your questions. I know this will be a long and difficult road but let me encourage you that you can get through it and you can be a better person for it. Just take one step at a time, get a plan of action and stick to it. Don't get discouraged and always ask questions. So, for now, I wish you good luck and may God guide your steps into your success.

NOTES

_____

_____

_____

_____

_____

_____

_____

_____

_____

_____

_____

_____

NOTES

Terminology

A

Accused: formally charged, but not yet tried for committing a crime; the person who has been charged may also be called the defendant.

Acquittal: a judgment of the court, based on the decision of either a jury or a judge who decides whether the person accused is not guilty of the crime for which he has been tried.

ADA: Assistant district attorney. An assistant district attorney works for the elected District Attorney. An ADA will review and prosecute cases as assigned. ADA's meet with law enforcement, witnesses, and victims. They generally have authority to dispose of those cases assigned to them.

Adjournment: putting off or postponing business or a session of the court until another time or place.

Adjudication: the judicial decision that ends a criminal proceeding by a judgment of acquittal, conviction, or dismissal of the case.

Affidavit: a written statement that the writer swears is true.

Aggravating Factors: factors that make a crime worse than most similar crimes. Aggravating factors are often defined by law and include such things as: victim's very old, gang related, done for hire, especially cruel, defendant does not support his family or took advantage of a position of trust.

Aggravated Range: When a person is sentenced, this indicates a sentence that is more severe than the "presumed" sentence for a given crime. A defendant may receive more time if the judge finds aggravating factors. If no aggravating factors are found, the sentence will come from either the "presumptive" or "mitigated" range.

Alleged: Said to be true, but not yet proven to be true; until the trial is over, the crime may be called the "alleged crime."

Appeal: A request by either the defense or the prosecution that a higher court review the results of a decision on certain motions or in a completed trial. This can be an appeal from superior court to an appeals court or an appeal from district court to superior court for a trial.

Arraignment: to bring a prisoner before a judge to ask how he pleads to the charges against him.

Arrest Warrant: A written order issued by the District court or magistrate including a statement of the crime of which the person to be arrested is accused, and directing that the person be arrested and held to answer the accusation before a magistrate or other judge.

Assailant: Person identified as the attacker.

B

Bail: An amount of money set by the court that allows a person charged with a crime to be released from custody. The purpose of bail is to ensure that the offender will return to court.

Bailiff: A uniformed officer who keeps order in the courtroom.

Bench: How the judge is sometimes referred to as in "the bench." This is also where the judge sits during the proceedings.

Bench Warrant: An order issued by a judge to bring to court an accused person who has been released before trial and does not return to court when ordered to do so; or a witness who has failed to appear when ordered to do so.

Beyond A Reasonable Doubt: The degree of proof needed for a jury or judge to convict an accused person of a crime.

Bond: In criminal court, a term meaning the same thing as "bail;" generally a certificate or evidence of a debt.

Bond Forfeiture: A hearing to determine if the bond on a defendant is to be forfeited after a defendant fails to show for court. Forfeited bond money goes to the public schools.

Bondsman: (Also Bail Bondsman) A licensed person or person working for a licensed company, who will post bond for a defendant upon payment of a fee. The fee is generally fifteen percent (15%) of the bond.

Booking: An official police record of the arrest of a person accused of committing a crime which identifies the accused, the time and place of arrest, the arresting authority, and the reason for the arrest.

C

Calendar: A document listing cases for hearing before a court. Calendars may be for the district court, superior court, motions, forfeitures, criminal docket management, plea, or trials.

Capital Case: This is a first-degree murder case in which the jury can impose either a life sentence or the death penalty. If a person is guilty of first-degree murder and there are any statutory aggravating factors then the State has to seek the death penalty.

Charge: The formal accusation filed by the prosecutor's office that a specific person has committed a specific crime; the filing may be called "pressing charges."

Clerk of Court: An officer of a court, this person keeps court records and seals, issues process, enters judgments and orders, gives certified copies from the records, etc.

Commitment: The warrant or order by which a court or magistrate directs an officer to take a person to prison.

Complaint: A term in civil cases that signifies a filing of a suit. In criminal court, the complaint is the reporting of a crime to authorities.

Concurrent Sentence: Running together; when two or more sentences are served at the same time. This is the opposite of a consecutive sentence.

Consecutive Sentence: Successive; succeeding one another in regular order; one sentence beginning at the completion of another.

Continuance: Postponement of a court hearing; putting it off until another day.

Criminal Court: A court that hears cases concerned with the alleged violation of criminal law.

Criminal Docket Management: A system used to review cases that have been taken to criminal superior court. Generally, an ADA meets with defense attorneys and reviews the strengths and weaknesses of a case. If no plea is worked out during CDM, cases are set for trial during CDM.

Criminal Justice System: The government agencies charged with law enforcement, prosecution of alleged violations of the criminal law, the court hearing of charges against the accused, and the punishment and supervision of those convicted.

Criminal Law: The law whose violation is considered an offense against the state and is punishable upon conviction by imprisonment and other penalties for adult offenders and by the action of a juvenile court for juvenile offenders.

Chromogenic Need: Indicators that determine what area of your life that may cause you to commit another criminal offense.

Cross Examination: The examination of a witness by the party opposed to the one who produced him during a trial or hearing, or upon taking a deposition.

CRS: Initials showing a case is in superior criminal court. CR is the designation for a case still in district court.

D

DA: Commonly refers to an attorney for the community elected by the people in his district to represent the interests of the general public, including crime victims, in court proceedings against people accused of committing crimes. Other jurisdictions use other terms: prosecutor, such as U.S. Attorney (a federal prosecutor), solicitor, or state's attorney.

Defendant: A person who has been formally charged with committing a crime; the person accused of a crime.

Defense Attorney: A lawyer who represents the defendant in legal proceedings. Victims are usually not required to speak with defense attorneys except in court, but may do so if they choose.

Defensive Driving School: An educational program taught by the community college that allows drivers who violate specific laws to attend a four-hour class designed to improve their driving skills. After completion of the course, violators are given a reduced plea.

Deferred Prosecution: Prosecution that the DA postpones for a certain period of time. The North Carolina Legislature has authorized District Attorneys to place defendants who commit offenses up to class H felonies on supervised probation with the agreement that the charges will be dismissed if probation is successfully completed. Defendants placed on deferred prosecution cannot have been on probation before. They are subject to all the regular conditions of probation such as paying restitution and community service. If the time elapses with no problems, the D A will dismiss the case.

Deferred Sentence: Defendant enters a guilty plea, receives probation for a certain amount of time, and gives up the right to trial. The DA dismisses the case if the probation is completed successfully.

Direct Examination: The first interrogation or examination of a witness during the trial by the party on whose behalf he is called.

Discovery: Process by which the DA provides to Defense Attorney information gathered during the investigation of a felony; the ascertainment of that which was previously unknown.

Dismissal: A decision by the prosecutor or another judicial officer to end a case for legal or other reasons.

Disposition: The final judicial decision which ends a criminal proceeding by a judgment of acquittal or dismissal, or which states the sentence if the accused is convicted.

District Attorney: Commonly refers to an official elected by the people of the community in his/her district to represent the interests of the general public, including crime victims, in court proceedings against people accused of committing crimes. Some jurisdictions use other terms: such as prosecutor, U.S. Attorney (a federal prosecutor), solicitor, or state's attorney.

District Attorney's Report: A report that is prepared by law enforcement in felony cases to inform the District Attorney what the facts are in a case. This is also known as a "felony report."

District Court: Where misdemeanor cases are heard concerning the violation of state statutes.

Double Jeopardy: Putting a person on trial more than once for the same offense; double jeopardy is forbidden by the U.S. Constitution.

E

Ex Parte: On one side only, done for one party.

Evidence: Testimony and objects used to prove statements made by the victim and the accused.

F

Failure To Appear (FTA): Defendant does not appear for court, order for arrest is issued.

Felony: A crime of a more serious nature than those designated as misdemeanors, carrying more potential jail time for an offender.

First Setting: The initial hearing for a case in the Criminal Docket Management process.

Final Setting: The final hearing for a case in the Criminal Docket Management process. Cases not disposed of during this setting are set for trial.

Fugitive: One who flees or escapes from some duty or penalty.

G

Grand Jury: A grand jury is composed of eighteen citizens meet in felony cases to determine whether a crime probably occurred and whether the defendant probably committed the crime. If twelve of the eighteen jurors agree then they return a true bill of indictment. The office of the District Attorney prepares indictments.

H

Hung Jury: A jury whose members cannot agree whether the accused is guilty or not; mistrial.

I

Impeach: To discredit the truthfulness of a witness.

Indictment: A formal written accusation made by a grand jury after submission by the prosecutor and filed in a court, alleging that a specific person committed a specific crime. The office of the District Attorney prepares indictments.

Indigent: An accused person who has been found by the court to be too poor to pay for his/her own attorney.

Infraction: Minor violations of the law that do not rise to the level of a misdemeanor. Driving offenses make up the bulk of charges designated as infractions.

Innocent: Free from guilt; free from legal fault. This should not be confused with the term "not guilty." Not guilty is a verdict by a judge or a jury that a person accused of a crime did not commit it or that there is not enough evidence to prove beyond a reasonable doubt that the accused committed the crime.

Investigation: The gathering of evidence by law-enforcement officials (and in some cases prosecutors) for presentation to a grand jury or in a court, to prove that the accused did commit the crime.

J

Jail: A confinement facility. Technically, a jail is administered by a local law-enforcement agency for adults and sometimes juveniles who have been accused of committing a crime but whose trials are not yet over, and persons who have been convicted and sentenced to imprisonment for one year or less; (see prison).

Judge: A judicial officer who has been elected or appointed to preside over a court of law.

Judgment: A court's final determination of the rights and obligations of the parties in a case. This may be in answer to a motion or trial.

Jury: A group of citizens who decide whether the accused is guilty or not. They are selected by law and sworn to determine certain facts by listening to testimony in order to reach a decision as to guilt or innocence.

Jury Selection: The process by which the judge, the prosecutor, and the defense attorney screen citizens who have been called to jury duty to determine if they will hear the evidence and decide guilt or innocence in a particular trial.

Juvenile: A person accused of an offense who is too young at the time of the alleged offense to be subject to criminal court proceedings as an adult and is therefore handled in the juvenile justice system.

L

LEO - Law Enforcement Officer

M

Magistrate: Person who can issue warrants when a person is accused of a crime. They are clothed with power as a public civil officer and have additional duties such as setting bond, hearing small claims, and accepting payment for certain infractions and misdemeanors.

Misdemeanor: Offenses lower than felonies and generally those punishable by fine or imprisonment otherwise than in a penitentiary.

These crimes are generally punishable by no more than 150 days in jail.

Mitigating Factor: A factor that makes a crime less deserving of punishment than most similar crimes. Mitigating factors are often defined by law and include such things as defendant was very young; the person was honorably discharged from the armed forces, etc.

N

Not Guilty: A verdict by a judge or a jury that a person accused of a crime did not commit it or that there is not enough evidence to prove beyond a reasonable doubt that the accused committed the crime.

Not Guilty Plea: A formal response by a person accused of committing a specific crime in which the accused says that the charges are not true and he did not commit the crime.

Notice: A written order to appear in court at a certain time and place.

O

Offender: An adult who has been convicted of a crime.

Offense: A crime; technically, in some jurisdictions, only the most minor crimes are called offenses.

Opening Statement: An outline of anticipated proof. Its purpose is to advise the jury prior to the testimony of the facts relied upon and of issues involved, and to give the jury a general picture of the facts and the situations so that the jury will be able to understand the evidence.

Order of Arrest: An order for the arrest of a defendant following the filing of charges or failure to appear when required by the court.

P

Parole: The conditional release of a convicted offender from a confinement facility before the end of his sentence with requirements for the offender's behavior set and supervised by a parole agency.

Penitentiary: A state or federal prison.

Perjury: Deliberate false testimony under oath involving a material fact.

Perpetrator: A person who actually commits a crime.

Personal Recognizance: The promise of an accused person to the court that he will return to court when ordered to do so; given in exchange for release before and during his trial.

Plea: A defendant's formal answer in court to the charge that he has committed a crime. Some possible plea's include: guilty, not guilty, no contest, or not guilty by reason of insanity.

Plea Bargain (Agreement): A plea agreed to by a defendant and the prosecutor; a negotiated plea that may set out exact terms relating to punishment and disposition of a case.

Probation: Conditional freedom granted to an offender by the court after conviction or guilty plea with requirements for the offender's behavior set and supervised by the court.

Probation Hearing: A hearing before a judge to review the performance of a defendant while on probation. Hearings are not generally held unless a probationer has violated some term of their probationary sentence.

Prosecutor: An attorney for the community elected by the voters of a district to represent the interests of the general public, including crime victims, in court proceedings against people accused of committing crimes. Some jurisdictions use other terms for the prosecutor, such as U.S. Attorney (a federal prosecutor), district attorney, or state's attorney.

Public Defender: An attorney employed by a government agency to represent defendants who are unable to hire private counsel.

R

Remand: To send back to a lower court. Typically refers to a situation where a Defendant in Superior Court asks to return a misdemeanor conviction to District Court for compliance with the judgment of that court.

Restitution: State law allows the prosecutor to request restitution (repayment for the victim's losses) as part of the sentence of any defendant who is found guilty of a crime. Reimbursable losses include out-of-pocket expenses (such as repair costs, medical bills, and stolen property) which have not previously been covered.

Retainer: The fee a defendant pays for an attorney to represent him.

Rights Of The Defendant: The powers and privileges which are constitutionally guaranteed to any person arrested and accused of committing a crime including: the right to remain silent; the right to an attorney at all stages of the proceedings; the right to a court-appointed attorney if the defendant does not have the financial means to hire her/his own counsel; the right to release on reasonable bail; the right to a speedy public trial by a jury or judge; the right to the process of the court to subpoena and produce witnesses; the right to see, hear and question the witnesses during the trial; and the right not to incriminate himself/herself.

RNA - A risk and needs assessment measures an offenders' criminal risk factors and specific needs that if addressed will reduce the likelihood of future criminal activity. An assessment instrument typically consists of a series of questions that help guide an interview with an offender in order to collect data on behaviors and attitudes that research indicates are related to the risk of recidivism. A total score is calculated using the risk and needs assessment instrument, and that score places the offender into a risk category (typically "low (level 4/5)," "moderate (level 2/3," or "high level 1)

S

Search Warrant: An order in writing, issued by a judge or magistrate, in the name of the state, directed to a sheriff, or another officer, commanding him to search a specific house, shop, or other premises, for specific property related to a crime.

Second Setting: The second court hearing during the Criminal Docket Management process.

Statute: An act of the legislature declaring, commanding, or prohibiting something a law.

Subpoena: A court paper requesting the appearance of a witness or documents to be present at a court proceeding.

Summons: A citation requiring a defendant to appear in court to answer a suit to which has been brought against him.

Superior Court: Where most felony cases are heard concerning violation of state statutes.

Suspect: a person who is believed by criminal justice officials to be one who may have committed a specific crime, but who has not been arrested or formally charged. Once arrested a suspect is called a defendant.

T

Testimony: Statements made in court by people who have sworn or affirmed, to tell the truth.

Transcript: In court, it is a verbatim writing of what was said in court during a trial, or a paper writing setting out terms of a plea taken from a defendant. Also a copy of an original writing or deed.

Trial: An examination of issues of fact and law before a judge and sometimes a jury at which evidence is presented to determine whether or not the accused person is guilty of committing a specific crime.

Traffic Court: An administrative court that hears only traffic matters, usually uncontested.

V

Verdict: The decision of a judge or jury at the end of a trial that the accused defendant is either guilty or not guilty.

W

Waiver: The intentional or voluntary relinquishment of a known right.

Warrant: See arrest warrant and bench warrant.

Witness: A person who has directly seen an event, such as a crime or who has other knowledge that is related to a court case; or something, such as a piece of physical evidence.

Writ Of Execution: A writ to put in force the judgment of decree of a court.

ABOUT THE AUTHOR

Wendy B. Sellars is a first-time author who picked this topic due to the current climate of our country. The fact that individuals are now more than ever hesitant about being stopped by law enforcement officers. Wendy wanted to make sure everyone was informed about their rights and how to handle an encounter with an LEO. Wendy wanted to ensure that your encounter with law enforcement ends in a positive way for both sides. As a career Probation Parole Officer and community activist, she uses her experience and passion for people to engage in this important conversation of how to navigate the criminal justice system.

Being employed with the Department of Public Safety for 20 years she has dedicated her life to helping individuals who have found themselves in the criminal justice system.

Wendy is a former member of the Thomasville Board of education and is currently serving on the Thomasville City

Council. She loves helping where she is needed and she is a member of several committees and organizations. Along with working with members of her community, she has also found a passion to work with individuals reentering the community.

Wendy Bryant Sellars was born in Manhattan, New York where she lived the majority of her childhood. She moved to Thomasville NC with her family in 1983. Wendy graduated from Thomasville High School in 1985 and enrolled at NC Central University that same year. Wendy graduated from NC Central University in 1989 with Bachelors of art in Political Science. Wendy held several jobs after graduating but her calling is working with people. Wendy began her love for working with the community early in college as she joined the amazing finer women of Zeta Phi Beta Sorority Inc. in 1988.

Connect Now on Social Media

- Facebook (Wendy Sellars)
- Instagram (4evagr8full)
- Twitter (Wendy Sellars)
- LinkedIn(Wendy Sellars

Email: theprocess911@yahoo.com

Disclaimer:

ie: The information in this publication is not the expressed view of the city of Thomasville, the Thomasville City Council or the Department of Public Safety wherein Wendy Sellars is affiliated.

References

1. "Probable Cause"
   www. criminal.findlaw.com
2. "You have been charged with a misdemeanor-what happens now?"
   www.the3rdjudicialdistrict.com
3. www.miranda.org

Disclaimer

The information contained in this book and these references are provided as a service to the reading community, and does not constitute legal advice. The author has tried to provide quality information but she makes no claims, promises or guarantees about the information provided or linked to these websites or its associated sites. Legal advice must be on a case by case basis and tailored to any specific circumstance of each case. Laws and information are constantly changing and nothing provided herein should be used as a substitution for the legal advice of a competent attorney.

NOTES

_____

_____

_____

_____

_____

_____

_____

_____

_____

_____

_____

_____

_____

_____

_____

_____

_____

_____

_____

_____

_____

_____

_____

_____

_____

_____

_____

_____

The Process

www.ingramcontent.com/pod-product-compliance
Lightning Source LLC
Chambersburg PA
CBHW051724170526
45167CB00002B/787